SENSES

Looking and seeing

Author's Note

I have worked alongside young children for more than forty years.
Over this period I have learned never to be surprised at their perceptive
comments about the physical world in which they live. Many of their
observations ('Have you seen the crinkles in the elephant's trunk?'
'How do seeds know which is their top and which is their bottom?')
indicate keen observation and an intuitive use of the senses of taste,
touch, sight, smell and hearing.

The sense-dependent nature of the young child should come as no
surprise to parents and teachers. In the early years of life images
provided by the senses shape our interpretation of our surroundings
and lay the foundations upon which subsequent learning is built.
The ideas of hot and cold, far and near, quiet and loud, sweet and sour,
soft and hard are developed through the interaction of the child with his
or her immediate environment. This interaction encourages observation
and questioning which in turn leads to talk and the extension and
deepening of language.

This book (like its companions in the series) is a picture book which seeks
to encourage both looking and talking. The text may be read by child or
adult. Alternatively it may be ignored, the pictures alone being used to
trigger an exploration of the child's own insights.

Paperback edition published 2000

© Franklin Watts 1997
Franklin Watts
96 Leonard Street
London EC2A 4XD

Franklin Watts Australia
14 Mars Road
Lane Cove
NSW 2066

ISBN: 0 7496 2571 6 (Hbk)
           0 7496 3786 2 (Pbk)

A CIP catalogue record for this book
is available from the British Library.

Dewey Decimal Classification Number: 612.8

Editor: Helen Lanz
Art Director: Robert Walster
Designer: Kirstie Billingham
Picture Research: Sarah Snashall

Printed in Malaysia

Picture credits

Commissioned photography by Steve Shott:
cover, title page, 4, 24.
Researched photography: Bruce Coleman Ltd
7 & 13 (H. Reinhard); The Image Bank 9 (J. Humer),
21 (J. Carmichael), 28 (J. Carmichael Jnr); Images
Colour Library 6, 10, 12, 16; NHPA 15 (J. Blossom),
18 & 25 (S. Dalton); Rex Features Ltd 5 (A. Griffiths)
17 (K. Andren), 26-27 (The Times);
Science Photo Library 14 (R. Planck); Telegraph
Colour Library 20 (A. Ponton); Tony Stone Images
11 (R. Wells), 19 (N. Parfitt), 29 (A. Wolfe); Zefa 8
(Eckstein), 23 (Krahmer).

SENSES

Looking and seeing

by Henry Pluckrose

FRANKLIN WATTS
LONDON • SYDNEY

4

We use our eyes to see
the things around us.

We see things
which move quickly
and things which stay quite still.

We see the slow,
dreamy movement of clouds,

and the sudden explosion
of fireworks.

We use our eyes to see
brilliant colours
and soft shadows.

Our eyes see
shapes and patterns –
on the wings of a butterfly
or the scales of a fish.

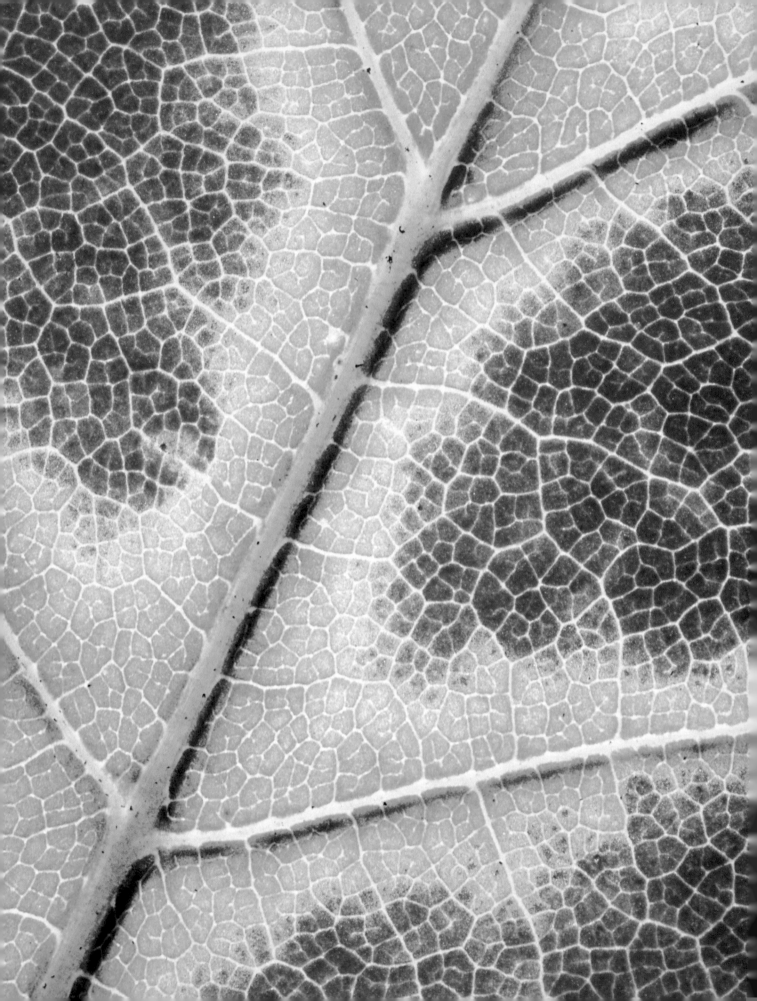

We see colour and pattern
on growing plants,
and in the texture of
lifeless brick and stone.

Our eyes can see
things far away
and things
that are close.

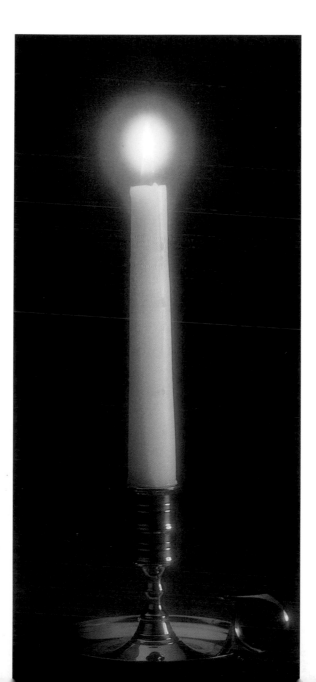

We can see things that are tiny
– and things that are large.

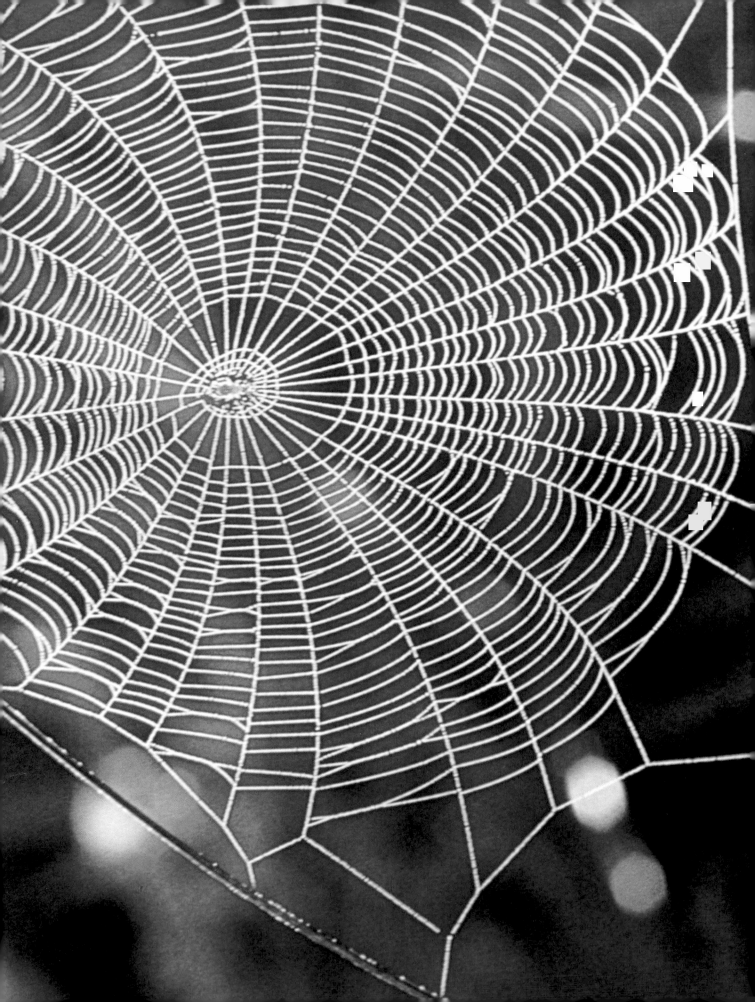

How well do you use your eyes?
Have you seen frost
on a spider's web,
or the delicate tracery
of a shell?

Have you noticed reflections
which dance on water,
or the silvery-blue shadows
of moonlight?

Sometimes things are so small
that our eyes cannot
see them clearly.
We may need a special glass
to make these things look bigger.

Often our senses work together.
Our eyes take messages
to our brain. We see the pig.
We may hear and smell it too!

Nearly all living creatures
have the sense of sight.
But some creatures
do not want to be seen.
They blend into the background.
This is called camouflage.

Without the sense of sight
we could not see.
Our world would be dark.
We could not see movement
or colour.

Investigations

This book has been prepared to encourage the young user to think about the sense of sight and the way in which we use our eyes. Each picture spread creates an opportunity for talk. Sharing talk with a sympathetic adult plays an important part in the development of a child's understanding of the world. Through the subtlety of language, ideas are formed, questioned and developed.

The theme of sight might be explored through questions like these:

⭐ Quick and slow (pp 6-9). What is the slowest movement we might notice . . . a sunflower turning its head through a day towards the sun? A snail crossing a concrete path? What things break suddenly from stillness to movement . . . a cat dashing across a road, a plane on a runway?

⭐ Colours (pp 10-15). What is red? How many different shades of red can you see around you? Are all reds (or blues, greens, yellows . . .) the same? How does a colour change when it falls into shade? How do we use colours in everyday life . . . what colours do we use for postboxes, fire engines, traffic lights, ambulances? Why have these colours been chosen?

⭐ Detail (pp 17-25). Our eyes can see an infinite number of images - far away and near at hand. Why does an object which is large (like an aircraft) look tiny in the sky? What fresh details appear when we examine a leaf or a piece of string under a magnifying glass?

⭐ Unity of senses (pp 26-27). It is important to provide opportunity to talk about the way in which our senses work together. What things do we know without seeing? (E.g. the smell of fresh bread leads us to the shelves without first seeing it.)

⭐ The world of nature (pp 28-29). Animals, too, need sight. How do animals use their eyes . . . for hunting, to watch for enemies, to find food? Do all living creatures have eyes which look forward (like ours)?

⭐ Blindness (pp 30-31). Sit with your eyes shut tight. Imagine. What would the world be like if you could not see?